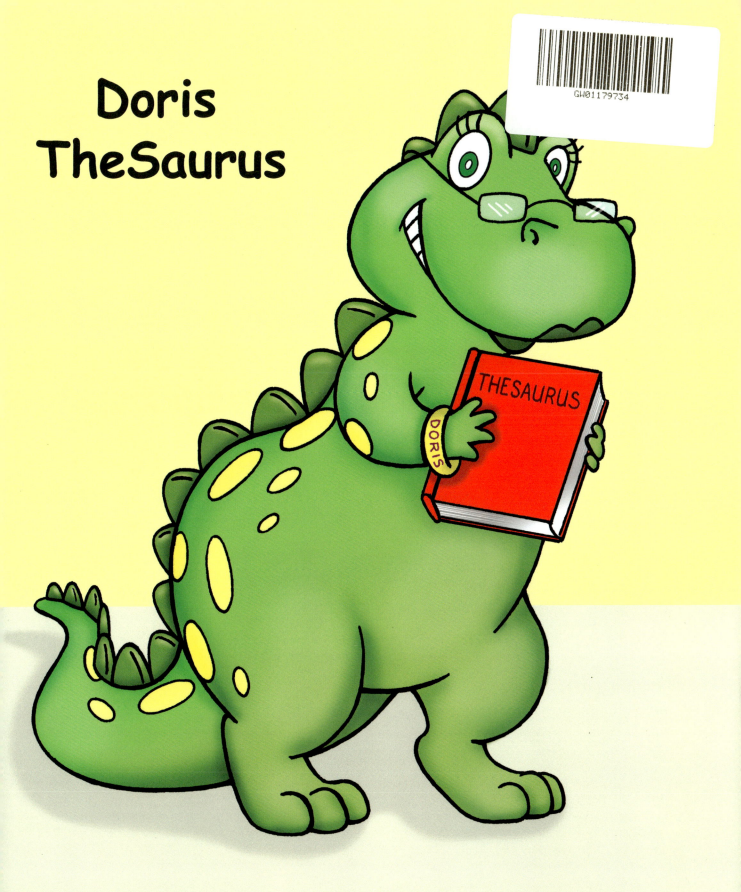

Doris TheSaurus

Maria L. Corkern

AuthorHouse™
1663 Liberty Drive, Suite 200
Bloomington, IN 47403
www.authorhouse.com
Phone: 1-800-839-8640

© 2008 Maria L. Corkern. All rights reserved.

No part of this book may be reproduced, stored in a retrieval system, or transmitted by any means without the written permission of the author.

First published by AuthorHouse 11/4/2008

ISBN: 978-1-4389-1436-7 (sc)

Library of Congress Control Number: 2008909020

Printed in the United States of America
Bloomington, Indiana

This book is printed on acid-free paper.

To James and Sara

Thanks to God, all of my family and friends for your inspiration, love and support throughout the years in all things.

Sara was having a difficult time
Trying to write a story.

Ms. Ross had assigned a challenging one,
So Sara turned to Cory.

"How do you do it?" she whispered to him.
"You make it look so easy."
"I got some help from a friend of mine
Who makes writing ... well ... breezy!"

"Who is your friend who knows so much?"
"Her name is Doris TheSaurus.
She showed me where to find new words
In a book that's called a *thesaurus!*"

"I've never heard of this thing," Sara said.
"It's strange and sounds like a creature."

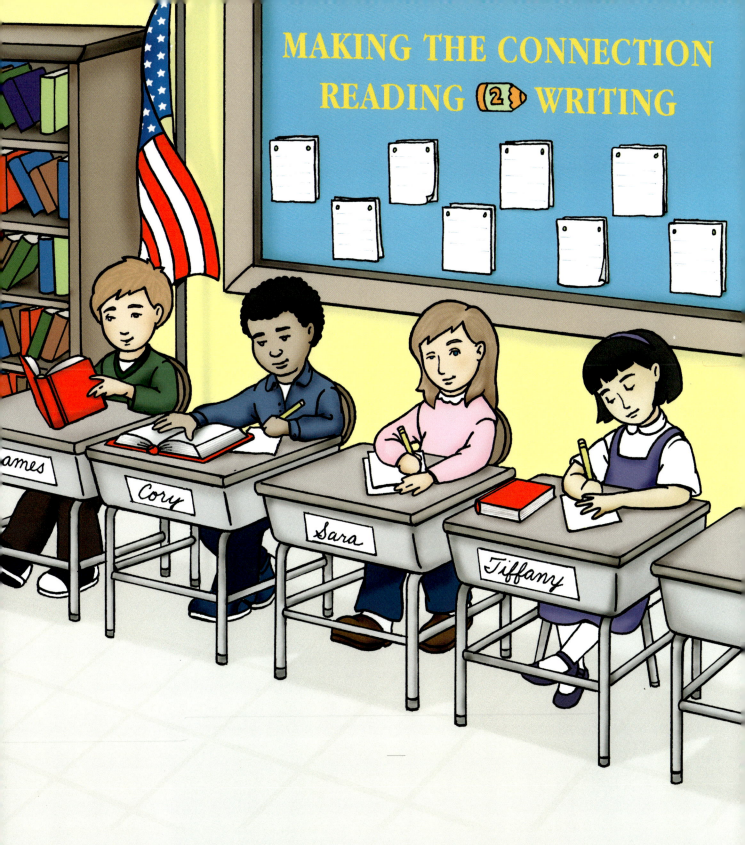

"No, not at all. It helps you out.
In a way, it's just like our teacher."

"Can I meet Doris?" she asked with hope.
"I want to see this book.

I want to have the very best writing,
And need to know where to look."

"Call her name, and she'll appear,"
Cory replied with a smile.
Sara just let the words spill out:
"Doris, *please* help me awhile."

All of a sudden the room was spinning
While words around her flew.
Then she heard a friendly, "Hello!"
From someone she thought she knew.

"You seem like Ms. Ross, but just not quite.
There's something about you that's weird."

"I'm Doris TheSaurus," the lady responded,
And then that new book appeared.

"Have you ever looked in these pages before?
You'll find words with similar meanings.

They're also known as synonyms.
They help you with writing *and* reading."

"Can I take a look in this book full of words?"
While over the cover she peered.
"That's why I came," Doris explained.
"Just choose a word, my dear."

Sara turned the pages quite fast,
And *big* was the word that she found.
Next to *big* was *enormous* and *huge*.
Her eyes grew wide and round.

"I'm starting to see how this book of yours works.
I look up a word that I wrote.
And then I read the ones that come next.
They'll help give my writing some hope."

"Exactly!" Doris squealed loudly with pride. "They're in alphabetical order.

Dictionaries work in much the same way. Just look at the pages' top borders."

Flipping the pages, Sara found words
She sometimes used in her writing.
Having this resource to give her ideas,
Her assignments seem much more exciting.

Happy: Delighted; Telling: Recited
Sara grinned up at her friend.
Hungry: Famished; Gone: Vanished
She wanted to read to the end!

"Whenever you find you need help with a word,
A thesaurus is where you could turn.
You'll find deeper meaning for words that you write."
"Thank you for helping me learn!"

When Doris was finished with all her assistance,
Words again swirled through the air.
Sara heard Doris say, "Call any time,"
As she found herself back in her chair.

"What did you find while you spent time with Doris?" Cory questioned his friend.

"Copious words to enhance my creations.
I can't wait to go back and amend!"

Then Sara knew that Ms. Ross had provided
This resource for her all along.
With special thanks to Doris TheSaurus,
Her writing will always be strong.

Thesaurus

Here are a few examples of how to replace commonly used words with more vivid words.

<u>**Big**</u>: enormous, huge, large, great, grand, colossal, immense, gigantic, vast, massive, tremendous, mighty, oversized, monstrous, humongous, gargantuan, jumbo, giant, mammoth, ginormous

Examples
Just Okay: The skillful hunter tracked the monster by following its big footprints in the soil.
Much Better: The skillful hunter tracked the monster by following its *massive* footprints in the soil.

<u>**Happy**</u>: delighted, glad, pleased, content, joyful, cheerful, blissful, ecstatic, cheery, jovial, satisfied, thrilled, overjoyed, elated, euphoric, jubilant, excited, tickled, thankful, cheerful

Examples
Just Okay: My language arts teacher was happy when she read my personal narrative.
Much Better: My language arts teacher was *delighted* when she read my personal narrative.

<u>**Held**</u>: embraced, hugged, cuddled, squeezed, gripped, grasped, clutched, clung

Examples
Just Okay: The little girl held her teddy bear as she fell asleep.
Much Better: The little girl *cuddled* her teddy bear as she fell asleep.

<u>**Looked**</u>: scanned, peered, glared, gazed, peeked, glimpsed, checked, searched, stared, watched, gaped, gawked, observed, viewed, inspected, scrutinized, analyzed, studied, examined

Examples
Just Okay: Grandma looked through the window, wondering when the rain would stop.
Much Better: Grandma *peered* through the window, wondering when the rain would stop.

Ran: scampered, hurried, dashed, darted, whizzed, rushed, zipped, zoomed, shot, sprinted, scuttled, hustled, flashed, charged, rushed, flew, fled, scrambled, scurried

Examples
Just Okay: The little, gray mouse ran across the floor.
Much Better: The little, gray mouse *scampered* across the floor.

Said: replied, answered, questioned, quipped, whispered, retorted, explained, exclaimed, echoed, acknowledged, yelled, cried, shouted, responded, murmured, giggled, sighed, hinted, inquired, queried, screamed, bellowed, complained, hollered, roared, clarified, enlightened, described, defended, asked, promised, guessed, ordered, scolded, raved, warned, mumbled, told

Examples
Just Okay: "I love my shiny new bike!" the boy said.
Much Better: "I love my shiny new bike!" the boy *exclaimed.*

Threw: tossed, flung, pitched, hurled, chucked, lobbed, flipped, launched

Examples
Just Okay: My neighbor wondered who threw the ball through his window.
Much Better: My neighbor wondered who *hurled* the ball through his window.

Walked: ambled, strolled, sauntered, moseyed, wandered, roamed, meandered, traveled, journeyed, strayed, trekked, hiked, marched, tramped, trampled, trudged, stepped, rambled, stomped

Examples
Just Okay: Enjoying the cool, morning breeze, Mama walked down the street.
Much Better: Enjoying the cool, morning breeze, Mama *strolled* down the street.

Lightning Source UK Ltd.
Milton Keynes UK
UKIC01n0151300713
214602UK00002B